[easy**sushi**]

RYLAND
PETERS
& SMALL

London New York

easysushi

emi kazuko

photography by peter cassidy

First published in the USA in 2000,
by **Ryland Peters & Small, Inc.**
519 Broadway, 5th Floor, New York NY 10012

10

Text © Emi Kazuko 2000
Design and photographs © Ryland Peters & Small 2000

Printed and bound in China

ISBN 1 84172 105 0

Author's Acknowledgments

I would like to thank those Japanese sushi chefs, past and present,
without whose devotion and hard work sushi would never have become
such a phenomenon the world over. My special thanks goes to my dear
friend Katsuko Hirose whose unceasing support and encouragement from
Japan have given me so much strength over the years. I would also like
to thank Elsa Petersen-Schepelern, for painstakingly editing this book.

Notes

All spoon measurements are level unless otherwise noted.
Uncooked or partly cooked eggs should not be served to the very old or frail,
the very young, or to pregnant women.
Specialty Japanese ingredients are available in larger supermarkets, Asian
markets, and through mail order sources [page 63].

Dedication

To my late parents who provided me with a good foundation in life and food.

Designer sailesh patel   **Senior Designer** louise leffler

Commissioning Editor elsa petersen-schepelern   **Editor** maddalena bastianelli

Production patricia harrington   **Art Director** gabriella le grazie   **Publishing Director** alison starling

Food Stylist emi kazuko   **Cooking Assistant** yasuko fukuoka   **Stylist** wei tang   **Photographer's Assistant** christian barnett

contents

introduction

Sushi, for many in the West a synonym for Japanese food, is a general term for all dishes using *sumeshi* [vinegared rice] in combination with other ingredients, mainly raw fish. However, sushi began life not in Japan, but in ancient Southeast Asia as a method for preserving fresh fish in steamed rice with salt.

Sushi was developed in its present form, based on vinegared rice, in the nineteenth century and flourished on street stalls in Edo, now Tokyo. It was the "fast food" of the time—and in many ways it still is. Many of my childhood memories are associated with my mother's sushi as a special lunch for school outings and theaters.

There are four main types:

1 Rice rolled in sun-dried nori seaweed with ingredients in the center [page 12], known as *maki-zushi* or *norimaki*.

2 Rice pressed in a mold, topped with cured or salted fish [page 31], known as *oshi-zushi* or *bo-zushi*.

3 "Fingers" of rice with a slice of fish, seafood, or omelet on top [page 46], known as *nigiri-zushi*.

4 Bowls of rice with other ingredients mixed through or arranged on top [page 50], known as *chirashi-zushi*.

All are easy to make at home as shown in this book, though *nigiri* is normally eaten at restaurants as it requires trained hands to mold rice to the right hardness so that the whole piece can be picked up easily, yet still loosen once in the mouth. In *Easy Sushi*, I have introduced some new ideas so you will be be able to have fun making sushi, using readily available ingredients as well as more authentic kinds. Many ingredients are now available in larger supermarkets and specialty food stores.

The key to success in handling rice is to treat it like a child: be gentle but firm with authority. Do not be put off at your first attempt; you need patience just as with children, and practice really does make perfect.

Sushi is ideal for parties too; rolled sushi *[norimaki]* and pressed sushi *[oshi-zushi]* can be made the day before and kept [at room temperature] until ready to serve. The lunchbox sushi mixture *[chirashi]* can also be prepared in advance and mixed with the other ingredients just before serving. Many sushi combinations are also suitable for vegetarians. Try sushi: you'll find it's easy.

ingredients

Japanese ingredients are becoming more widely available in supermarkets and specialty food stores, but can certainly be found in Asian markets. This directory will help you identify them.

shoyu
[Japanese soy sauce]

mirin
[Japanese sweet rice wine, for cooking only]

su
[Japanese rice vinegar]

sake
[Japanese rice wine]

nori
[sheets of dried seaweed]

kanpyo
[dried gourd ribbons]

kombu
[dried kelp for cooking rice]

white sesame seeds

black sesame seeds

renkon, sliced
[lotus root]

shiso leaf
[Japanese herb, also known as perilla]

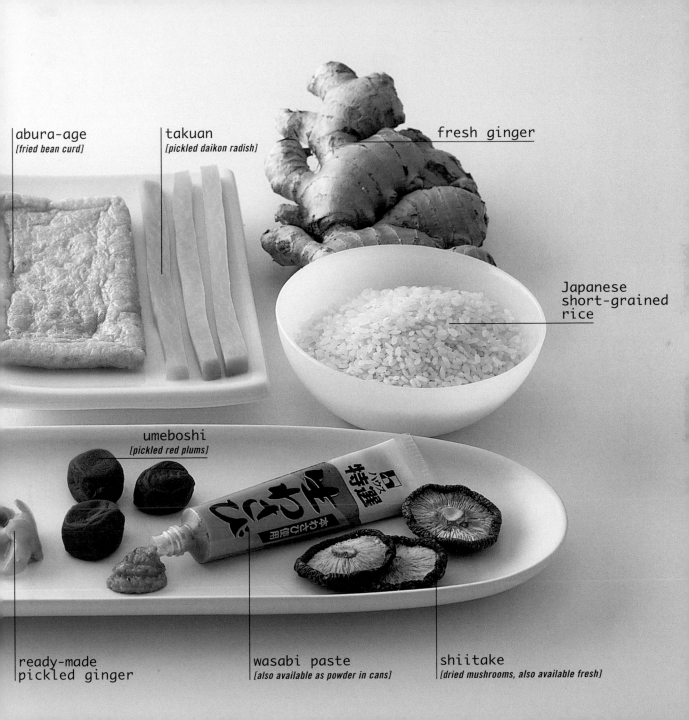

abura-age
[fried bean curd]

takuan
[pickled daikon radish]

fresh ginger

Japanese
short-grained
rice

umeboshi
[pickled red plums]

ready-made
pickled ginger

wasabi paste
[also available as powder in cans]

shiitake
[dried mushrooms, also available fresh]

Sushi is a general term for all food with *"sumeshi,"* or vinegared rice. Remember—sushi should never be put in the fridge [it will go hard.] The vinegar will help preserve it for a few days if kept, wrapped, in a cool place, such as a shady windowsill. To make sushi rice, boil 15 percent more water than rice. Don't take the lid off during cooking, or you will spoil the rice.

vinegared rice sumeshi

1¾ cups Japanese-style short-grained rice
1 piece of dried kelp *[kombu]*, 2 inches square, for flavoring [optional]
3 tablespoons Japanese rice vinegar
2½ tablespoons sugar
2 teaspoons sea salt

Makes 4 cups

1   Put the rice in a large bowl and wash it thoroughly, changing the water several times, until the water is clear. Drain and leave in the strainer for 1 hour. If short of time, soak the rice in clear, cold water for 10–15 minutes, then drain.

2   Transfer to a deep, heavy-bottom saucepan, add 2 cups water and a piece of dried kelp *[kombu],* if using. Cover and bring to a boil over a high heat, about 5 minutes. Discard the kelp.

3   Lower the heat and simmer, covered, for about 10 minutes, or until all the water has been absorbed. Do not lift the lid. Remove from the heat and leave, still covered, for about 10–15 minutes.

4   Mix the rice vinegar, sugar, and salt in a small pitcher and stir until dissolved.

5   Transfer the cooked rice to a large, shallow dish or *handai* [Japanese wooden *sumeshi* tub]. Sprinkle generously with the vinegar dressing.

6   Using a wooden spatula, fold the vinegar dressing into the rice. Do not stir. While folding, cool the rice quickly using a fan. Let the rice cool to body temperature before using to make sushi.

Wonderful party food, nori rolls [norimaki] are probably the best-known sushi of all. A sheet of nori seaweed is spread with sushi rice, a line of filling put down the middle, then the sheet is rolled up into a cylinder. The cylinder is cut into sections before serving. All ingredients are sold in Asian shops and larger supermarkets.

simple rolled sushi norimaki

¾ quantity vinegared rice
    [page 11]

Hand vinegar:
¼ cup Japanese rice vinegar
1 cup water

For rolling:
8–inch piece unwaxed
    cucumber, or 2–3 kirby
    cucumbers, unpeeled
3 sheets nori seaweed
wasabi paste or powder

To serve:
pickled ginger
extra wasabi paste
Japanese soy sauce [shoyu]

a sushi rolling mat [makisu]

Makes 6 rolls
[36 pieces]

1   Prepare the vinegared rice [sumeshi] as in the previous recipe. Mix the hand vinegar ingredients in a small bowl and set aside.

2   To prepare the cucumber, cut into quarters lengthwise, then cut out the seeds and cut the remainder, lengthwise, into ½-inch square matchstick lengths. You need 6 strips, each with some green skin.

3   Just before assembling, pass the nori over a very low gas flame or electric hotplate, just for a few seconds to make it crisp and bring out the flavor. Cut each sheet in half crosswise.

4   Assemble the sushi according to the method on the following pages.

5   Cut each roll into 6 pieces, as shown on page 14–15.

6   Arrange on a serving plate and serve with pickled ginger, a little pile of wasabi paste, and a dish of Japanese soy sauce.

Make the vinegared rice *[sumeshi],* prepare and assemble the ingredients.

1   Put a sushi rolling mat *[makisu]* on your work surface, then put half a sheet of toasted nori seaweed on top. Dip your hands in the bowl of hand vinegar, then take a handful of the rice [2–3 heaped tablespoons] in your hands and make into a log shape. Put the rice in the center of the nori.

2   Using your fingers, spread it evenly all over, leaving about ½-inch margin on the far side. [The rice will stick to your hands, so dip them in the hand vinegar as necessary.]

3   Take a small dot of wasabi paste on the end of your finger and draw a line down the middle across the rice, leaving a light green shadow on top of the rice [not too much— wasabi is very hot!]

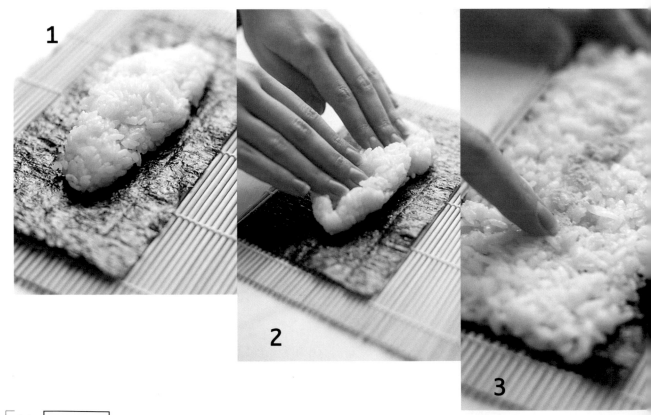

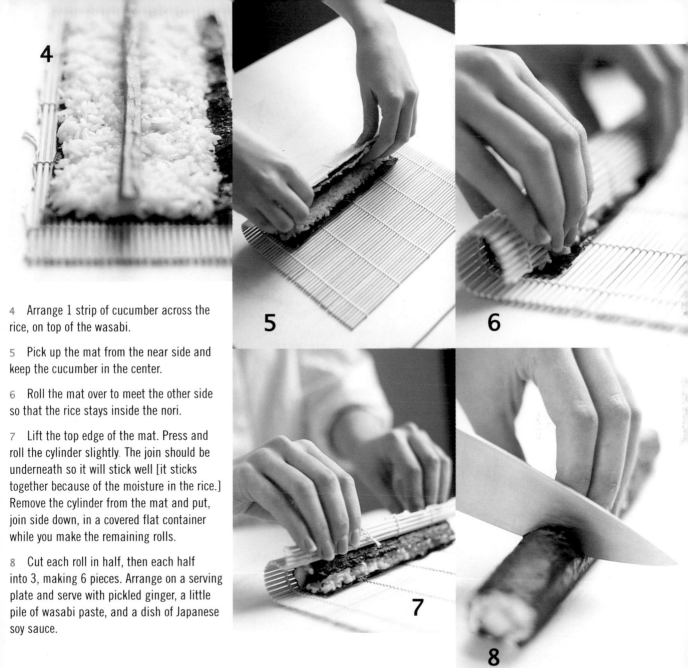

4   Arrange 1 strip of cucumber across the rice, on top of the wasabi.

5   Pick up the mat from the near side and keep the cucumber in the center.

6   Roll the mat over to meet the other side so that the rice stays inside the nori.

7   Lift the top edge of the mat. Press and roll the cylinder slightly. The join should be underneath so it will stick well [it sticks together because of the moisture in the rice.] Remove the cylinder from the mat and put, join side down, in a covered flat container while you make the remaining rolls.

8   Cut each roll in half, then each half into 3, making 6 pieces. Arrange on a serving plate and serve with pickled ginger, a little pile of wasabi paste, and a dish of Japanese soy sauce.

Other ingredients traditionally used for rolled sushi in Japan include *kanpyo* [dried gourd ribbons], tuna with scallion, *natto* [steamed fermented soy beans], chile-marinated cod's roe, and salted plum [*umeboshi*] with shiso herb. You can also make variations using ingredients more readily available in the West.

rolled sushi variations

¾ quantity vinegared rice
[page 11]
3 sheets nori seaweed

Hand vinegar:
¼ cup Japanese rice
vinegar
1 cup water

Filling:
4 oz. fresh salmon, skinned
2½ inches pickled daikon
[takuan], cut lengthwise
into ½-inch square sticks
4–6 fresh shiso leaves or
6–8 basil leaves
2 small red salted plums
[umeboshi], pitted and
torn in pieces
wasabi paste

To serve:
pickled ginger
extra wasabi paste
Japanese soy sauce [shoyu]

a sushi rolling mat
[makisu]

Makes 36 pieces

1   Make the vinegared rice [*sumeshi*] following the recipe on page 11. Mix the hand vinegar ingredients in a small bowl.

2   Cut the piece of salmon into ½-inch square sticks. To make a salmon sushi, follow the method on the previous page, using a row of salmon strips instead of cucumber. [Enough to make 2 rolls.]

3   To make a pickled daikon sushi, follow the method on the previous page, using 3 strips of pickled daikon in a row instead of cucumber, and omitting the wasabi paste. [Enough to make 2 rolls.]

4   To make the pickled plum sushi, follow the method on the previous page, using the shiso or basil leaves and the pieces of plum. [Enough to make 2 rolls.]

5   Cut each roll into 6 pieces, then arrange on a plate and serve with pickled ginger, a mound of wasabi paste, and a dish of soy sauce.

Variation:
You can also leave the salmon fillet whole, then lightly broil it for about 2 minutes on each side. Cool, put in a bowl, flake with a fork, then stir in 2 finely chopped scallions. Mix in 2 teaspoons mayonnaise, salt, and pepper, then proceed as in the main recipe.

big sushi rolls futomaki

Thick nori rolls normally contain 5 ingredients with contrasting colors, all wrapped up in a whole sheet of nori. A little difficult to eat, but a beautiful party dish.

1 quantity vinegared rice [page 11]
3 sheets nori seaweed

Hand vinegar:
¼ cup rice vinegar
1 cup water

Fillings:
9–12 uncooked jumbo shrimp, unpeeled
4 eggs
¼ cup sugar
8 oz. spinach, about 2 cups leaves
3½ tablespoons Japanese soy sauce [shoyu]
1 oz. dried gourd [kanpyo] or 1 carrot, cut into ⅛-inch square shreds
5–6 dried shiitake mushrooms
1 tablespoon mirin [rice wine] or sweet sherry
salt

To serve:
pickled ginger
Japanese soy sauce [shoyu]

a sushi rolling mat [makisu]

Makes 3 rolls [24 pieces]

1   Make the vinegared rice following the recipe on page 11. Mix the hand vinegar ingredients in a small bowl and set aside.

2   Skewer a toothpick through each length of shrimp to prevent curling while cooking. Blanch in boiling water for 3 minutes until firm and pink. Immediately plunge into cold water and drain. Remove and discard the toothpicks, shells, and dark back vein.

3   Using the eggs, 2 tablespoons of the sugar, and a pinch of salt, make an omelet following the method on page 60. Let cool, then cut lengthwise into ½-inch wide strips.

4   Blanch the spinach in lightly salted water for 1 minute. Plunge into cold water. Drain and pat dry with paper towels. Sprinkle with 2 teaspoons soy sauce and set aside.

5   If using kanpyo, rub it with salt and a little water, then soak in water for 10 minutes and drain. Cut into 8-inch lengths. Soak the shiitake in warm water for 30 minutes, then drain, retaining the soaking water. Cut the shiitake into 2-inch strips. Put 1 cup of the soaking liquid in a small saucepan with 3 tablespoons soy sauce, 2 tablespoons of the sugar, and the mirin or sherry. Bring to a boil. Add the kanpyo or carrot shreds and shiitake strips. Simmer over a low heat for 15 minutes. Let cool in the liquid and set aside.

6   Toast the nori over a hotplate or gas flame and arrange, crosswise, one whole sheet at a time, on a sushi rolling mat, following the method on page 16. Dip your hands in the hand vinegar. Take one-sixth of the rice and squeeze it into a firm ball. Put the rice ball on one side of the nori sheet in the center and, using wet fingers, spread evenly over the half side of nori, leaving about 1-inch margin on the far side. Repeat this once more to fill the other half. The rice layer should be fairly thick—add extra rice if necessary.

7   Arrange 3–4 shrimp in a row across the rice about 2 inches from the front edge. Add a row of omelet strips and a row of spinach on top of the shrimp. Add a row of kanpyo or carrot and a row of shiitake on top, so that all 5 ingredients are piled in the center of the rice, like logs of timber. Each roll should use one-third of each ingredient.

8   Pick up the mat from the near side and, keeping all the ingredients in the center, roll the mat following the method on page 14–15. Remove the mat and put the roll on a plate, join-side down. Repeat to make 2 more rolls.

9   Cut each roll into 8 and serve with little dishes of soy sauce and pickled ginger.

This battleship-shaped version of *nigiri*—*zushi* has a ribbon of nori seaweed wrapped vertically around the rice and raw toppings such as *ikura* [salmon caviar] and sea urchin. This recipe includes Western variations using crab lumpmeat and flaked crabmeat.

battleship rolls
gunkanmaki

½ quantity vinegared rice [page 11]
1½ sheets nori seaweed

Hand vinegar:
¼ cup vinegar
1 cup water

Toppings:
½–⅔ cup crabmeat
about 1 teaspoon sake
2 teaspoons wasabi paste or powder
¼–⅓ cup salmon caviar [ikura]
   or red lumpfish caviar
12 pickled caper berries or capers

To serve:
pickled ginger
Japanese soy sauce [shoyu]

Makes 12

Use the "fresh" lump crabmeat sold in a tub by your local fish store, not the pasteurized canned variety.

1   Make the vinegared rice [*sumeshi*] following the method on page 11. Mix the hand vinegar ingredients in a small bowl.

2   Put the crabmeat on a small plates and sprinkle with a little sake. If using wasabi powder, mix 1–2 teaspoons powder in an egg cup with about 1–2 teaspoons water to make a clay-like consistency. Turn it upside down and set aside to prevent it drying out.

3   Cut each sheet of nori crosswise into ribbons, 7 x 1 inches, making 12 ribbons in total.

4   Dip your hands in the vinegar mixture, then take about 1–2 tablespoons rice in one hand and squeeze it into a rectangular mound about 2 x ¾ x 1¼ inches high. Wrap a nori ribbon around it, overlapping about 1 inch at the end. Glue it together with a grain of vinegared rice. Put 2 teaspoons caviar and a few pickled caper berries or capers on top. Repeat to make 3 more rolls with caviar, 4 with crabmeat topped with a little salmon caviar, and 4 with crabmeat with a dot of wasabi on top.

5   Arrange on a platter, and serve with the pickled ginger and a small dish of soy sauce as party food. If making individual servings, serve the soy sauce in small, separate dishes.

½ quantity vinegared rice
   [page 11]
4 frilly lettuce leaves, such as
   oak leaf
4 Boston lettuce leaves
4 small iceberg lettuce leaves
Japanese soy sauce [shoyu],
   to serve

Hand vinegar:
¼ cup rice vinegar
1 cup water

Toppings:
3 oz. smoked fish, such as
   trout or haddock
1 bay leaf
1 teaspoon sugar
3 oz. smoked salmon, finely
   chopped
1 tablespoon lemon juice
¼–⅓ cup black lumpfish
   caviar
1 tablespoon caper berries or
   capers, drained

Makes 12

1   Make the vinegared rice *[sumeshi]* following the method on page 11. Mix the hand vinegar ingredients in a small bowl and set aside.

2   Put the smoked trout or haddock and bay leaf in a saucepan, cover with boiling water, return to a boil, then simmer for 5 minutes or until cooked. Drain well. Remove and discard the skin and all the small bones. Put in a bowl and flake finely with a fork. Stir in the sugar and let cool.

3   Sprinkle the smoked salmon with lemon juice.

4   Cut a 1-inch wide strip crosswise from the top of the frilly leaves and Boston lettuce leaves. Make a small cup, 3-inches diameter, from the inner iceberg leaves.

5   Make 12 rectangular mounds of rice, following the method on page 20. Instead of wrapping in nori, wrap 4 in frilly lettuce leaves, 4 in Boston lettuce leaves, and 4 in iceberg lettuce cups. Put 1–1½ tablespoons of fish flakes on top of the rice in the frilly lettuce. Put about 1–1½ tablespoons smoked salmon on the rice in the Boston lettuce, and about 1–1½ tablespoons caviar in the iceberg cups. Top the smoked fish with a little caviar, the salmon with a caper berry or caper, and the caviar with a few flakes of smoked fish.

6   Arrange on a platter or small plates and serve with a small dish of soy sauce.

Battleship rolls can be made with lettuce leaves instead of nori. Use flexible leaves from Boston lettuce or leaf lettuce as ribbons, and small inner leaves from an iceberg as cups.

lettuce rolls

Uramaki is an "inside-out" roll, with nori inside and rice outside. This shrimp tempura version is popular in restaurants—the nori prevents the vinegar in the rice and the oil in the tempura from touching each other. The unlikely combination of two opposing tastes makes a surprisingly delicious match.

inside-out sushi
uramaki

¼ quantity vinegared rice [page 11]
2 sheets nori seaweed
pickled ginger, to serve

Hand vinegar:
2 tablespoons rice vinegar
½ cup water

Tempura shrimp:
8 uncooked jumbo shrimp, 4 peeled completely, 4 left with tail fins intact, deveined
⅔ cup all-purpose flour, sifted
¼ cup sesame seeds, black or white
salt
sunflower oil, for frying

8 toothpicks or bamboo skewers
a sushi rolling mat [makisu] covered with plastic wrap

Makes 20 pieces [4 rolls]

1 Make the vinegared rice [sumeshi] following the method on page 11 and divide into 4. Mix the hand vinegar ingredients in a small bowl. Skewer a toothpick through each shrimp from top to tail to prevent curling while cooking.

2 Cover one side of a sushi rolling mat [makisu] with plastic wrap and put it on a dry cutting board, plastic side up.

3 Fill a wok or deep saucepan one-third full of oil and heat to 340°F or until a cube of bread browns in about 60 seconds. To make the tempura batter, put ½ cup water in a bowl, sift the flour into the water, and mix with a fork. One by one, dip the shrimp in the batter, then fry in the hot oil for 3–4 minutes or until golden-brown. Remove and drain on paper towels and carefully remove and discard the toothpicks.

4 Put the nori on a completely dry cutting board. Dip your hands in the hand vinegar. Take a handful of the rice [2–3 heaped tablespoons] in your hands and make into a log shape. Put the rice in the center of the nori. Using your fingers, spread it evenly all over, right to the edges. Sprinkle 1 tablespoon sesame seeds all over the rice.

5 Turn the whole thing over onto the plastic-covered mat.

6 Arrange 2 tempura shrimp down the center of the nori, with the tails sticking out at the ends [you can remove the tail fins if preferred.]

7 Roll the mat following the method on page 14–15. Remove from the mat and repeat to make 3 more rolls, using black or white sesame seeds.

8 Cut each roll into 5 pieces and arrange on a platter. Serve with pickled ginger and a little soy sauce in a small dish beside the platter or in small individual plates.

A perfect sushi for parties. Serve the rice, nori sheets, and prepared ingredients on plates and let people roll their own. Choose ingredients with varied tastes and colors. This is a delicious variation of the hand roll—using smoked salmon instead of crabsticks.

smoked salmon hand rolls temaki

¾ quantity vinegared rice
  [page 11]
4 sheets nori seaweed
  or 8 salad leaves
pickled ginger, to serve

Hand roll fillings:
4 oz. smoked salmon
4 scallions
2½ inches pickled daikon
  [takuan] or cucumber
1 avocado
juice of 1 lemon

Makes 8 rolls

1 Make the vinegared rice [sumeshi] following the method on page 11.

2 Cut the smoked salmon lengthwise into ⅛-inch strips.

3 Finely slice the scallions lengthwise into 3–4-inch strips. Slice the pickled daikon or cucumber thinly.

4 Cut the avocado in half, remove the pit, and peel carefully. Thinly slice the flesh and brush with lemon juice.

5 Toast the nori sheets by quickly passing over a low flame to make them crisp and bring out the flavor. Cut each sheet in half crosswise.

6 Put the rice in a serving bowl and arrange salmon, scallion, and avocado on a serving platter. Put the nori and pickled ginger on small separate plates .

7 To assemble, follow the step-by-step directions on the following page.

ASSEMBLING HAND ROLLS

2 Arrange your choice of fillings diagonally over the rice from the center to the outer corner.

1 Take one piece of nori seaweed in one hand and add 2–3 tablespoons of vinegared rice *[sumeshi]*. Spread the rice over one half of the nori.

4

3

3   Take the bottom right-hand corner and curl it towards the middle to form a cone.

4   Keep rolling the cone until complete. To glue the cone closed [optional], put a few grains of rice on the edge of the nori, and press together.

5   When the cone is complete, add your choice of a few drops of soy sauce, a few pieces of pickled ginger, and a dab of wasabi paste.

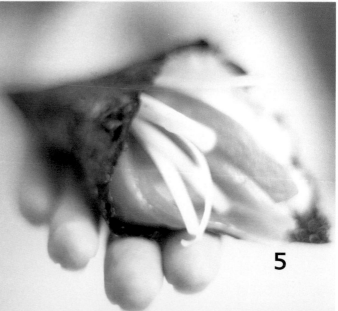

5

Battera, a speciality from Osaka, is one of the most popular sushi in Japan. It is made in a container or molded into a log with a sushi mat and cut into small pieces. In restaurants and stores it often comes wrapped up with a transparent sheet of kombu [dried kelp].

mackerel sushi pieces
battera

10 oz. mackerel fillet
3–4 tablespoons rice vinegar
salt
½ quantity vinegared rice [page 11]

Hand vinegar:
2 tablespoons rice vinegar
½ cup water

To serve:
pickled ginger
Japanese soy sauce [shoyu]

a wooden mold or rectangular plastic container, 7 x 4½ x 2 inches

Makes 1 battera [16 pieces]

1   Start the preparation for this dish a few hours before cooking the rice. Take a dish larger than the fish fillets and cover with a thick layer of salt. Put the mackerel fillets, flesh side down, on top of the salt and cover completely with more salt. Set aside for 3–4 hours. Remove the mackerel and rub off the salt with damp paper towels. Carefully remove all the bones with tweezers, then put into a dish and pour the rice vinegar over the fillets. Leave to marinate for 30 minutes.

2   Make the vinegared rice [sumeshi] following the recipe on page 11. Mix the hand vinegar ingredients in a small bowl and set aside.

3   Using your fingers, carefully remove the transparent skin from each fillet, starting at the tail end. Put the fillets, skin side down, on a cutting board and slice off the highest part from the center of the flesh so the the fillets will be fairly flat. Keep the trimmings.

4   Line a wet wooden mold or rectangular container with a large piece of plastic wrap.

5   Put a fillet, skin side down, in the mold or container. Fill the gaps with the other fillet and trimmings. Dip your fingers in the hand vinegar, then press the cooked rice down firmly on top of the fish. Put the wet wooden lid on top, or fold in the plastic and put a piece of cardboard and a weight on top.

6   You can leave it in a cool place [not the refrigerator] for a few hours. When ready to serve, remove from the container and unwrap any plastic. Take a very sharp knife and wipe it with a vinegar-soaked cloth or piece of paper towel. Cut the block of sushi in 4 lengthwise, then in 4 crosswise, making 16 pieces in all.

7   Arrange on a plate, and serve with pickled ginger and a little soy sauce in small individual dishes.

PRESSED SUSHI

masu-zushi smoked fish sushi

This *oshi-zushi* [pressed sushi] or its rolled equivalent, *bo-zushi* [log sushi] will keep for up to 36 hours—as a result, they are the best-selling items at all Japanese airports. Travelers buy them for Japanese friends living abroad as a reminder of the true taste of Japan. They are easy to make and can be made the day before.

1   Make the vinegared rice *[sumeshi]* following the method on page 11. Mix the hand vinegar ingredients in a small bowl and set aside.

2   Lay the smoked trout or salmon slices evenly in the bottom of a wet wooden mold. Alternatively, use a rectangular container lined with a piece of plastic wrap large enough for the edges to hang out of the container.

3   Wet your hands in the hand vinegar, transfer the vinegared rice into the mold and press it firmly and evenly into the mold. Put the wet wooden lid on top. If using a plastic container, fold in the plastic wrap to cover the rice and top with a piece of cardboard just big enough to cover the rice, and put a weight on top. Leave in a cool place [but never the refrigerator] for 2–3 hours or overnight.

4   When ready to serve, remove from the container and unwrap any plastic. Take a very sharp knife and wipe it with a vinegar-soaked cloth or piece of paper towel. Cut the sushi into 4 lengthwise, then in 4 crosswise, making 16 pieces.

5   Arrange on a large serving plate. Put a fan-shaped piece of lemon on top. Serve with pickled ginger and a little Japanese soy sauce.

½ quantity vinegared rice [page 11]

Hand vinegar:
2 tablespoons rice vinegar
½ cup water

Toppings:
6 oz. smoked trout or smoked salmon,
   thickly sliced
2 slices lemon, cut into 16 fan-shaped pieces

To serve:
pickled ginger
Japanese soy sauce *[shoyu]*

*a wooden mold or rectangular plastic
   container, 7 x 4½ x 2 inches*

Makes 1 block [16 pieces]

1   Make the vinegared rice *[sumeshi]* following the method on page 11.

2   Put the fish in a saucepan, add just enough boiling water to cover, and simmer until well-cooked. Drain, then carefully remove all the small bones. Pat dry with paper towels and return to the dry saucepan. Using a fork, crush into fine flakes. Add the sugar and a pinch of salt, then cook over a low heat, continuously stirring with a fork, for about 2 minutes, or until the fish is very dry and flaky. If using red food coloring, dilute 1 drop with 1 tablespoon water, then stir quickly through the fish to spread the color evenly. Remove from the heat and let cool. [Alternatively, use fresh salmon cooked to flakes in the same way or crush canned cooked red salmon into flakes.]

3   Bring a small saucepan of lightly salted water to a boil, add the peas, and cook for 5 minutes or until soft. Drain and pat dry with paper towels. Crush with a mortar and pestle or in a food processor to form a smooth green paste. Stir in the sugar and a pinch of salt.

4   Lightly oil a small saucepan and heat over a moderate heat. Put the eggs, milk, and sugar in a bowl, mix, then pour into the pan. Quickly stir with a fork to make soft scrambled eggs. Remove from the heat and let cool.

5   Divide the vinegared rice into three. To make the cherry blossom sushi, put 1 tablespoon of the pink fish flakes in the bottom of a small heart-shaped mold and press 1 tablespoon rice on top. Turn out onto a plate, fish side up. Repeat until all the pink flakes and a third of the rice are used. Using a second mold, repeat using the green pea paste and another third of the rice. Using a third mold, repeat using the scrambled eggs with the remaining third of the rice. If using grilled fresh salmon, use a fourth mold.

6   Arrange cherry blossom, flower, star, and spring green sushi on a large serving plate.

½ quantity vinegared rice [page 11]

Cherry blossom sushi:
4 oz. cod or haddock fillet, skinned
2 tablespoons sugar
salt and pepper
red food coloring*

Spring green sushi:
4 oz. frozen peas
2 teaspoons sugar
salt

Golden star sushi:
2 eggs, beaten
1 tablespoon milk
1 tablespoon sugar

star, daisy, star, and heart-shaped
sushi molds, or cookie cutters

Makes 18-20 pieces

* If you don't want to use the food coloring, use broiled fresh salmon, flaked, instead of the white fish and coloring.

stars, hearts, and flowers

Just like cookies, these children's sushi are made in pretty colors and shapes. Specially shaped molds are sold in Japanese stores, but if you don't have access to such markets, use decorative cookie cutters and other mold shapes.

children's favorites

¾ quantity vinegared rice
[page 11]
3 sheets nori seaweed
Japanese soy sauce
[shoyu], to serve

Hand vinegar:
¼ cup Japanese rice
vinegar
1 cup water

Fillings:
1 egg, beaten
2 tablespoons sugar
2½ inches carrot, sliced
lengthwise into
⅛-inch sticks
2 thin hot dogs, 7 inches
long, or 4 Vienna
sausages, 4 inches long
2½ inches unwaxed
cucumber
or 1 kirby cucumber
3 oz. canned red salmon,
drained
1 tablespoon mayonnaise
salt
sunflower oil, for frying

*a Japanese omelet pan or
8-inch nonstick skillet*
*a sushi rolling mat
[makisu]*

Makes 6 rolls
[36 pieces].

Sushi is fun when you make it for or with children. Devising sushi for non-Japanese kids led me to a surprise discovery of a match such as sausages and fish fingers with vinegared rice. Let's start with simple "sausage rolls."

1   Make vinegared rice following the method on page 11. Mix the hand vinegar ingredients in a bowl.

2   Strain the egg into a small bowl, add ½ tablespoon sugar and a pinch of salt, and beat until dissolved. Heat a skillet, brush with sunflower oil, and rub off any excess with paper towels.

3   Pour in the egg mixture and spread evenly by tilting the skillet to make a thin pancake. Prick any bubbles with a fork and fill any holes with egg by tilting the skillet. After 30 seconds, turn the omelet over for 30 seconds to dry the other side and make it golden yellow. Remove from the heat, remove with a spatula, put on a cutting board, and cut in half.

4   Blanch the carrot in about 1 cup boiling salted water at a high heat for 2–3 minutes. Lower the heat and stir in 1½ tablespoons sugar and a pinch of salt. Simmer for another 2–3 minutes, then remove from the heat and let cool in the juice.

5   Put half the omelet on a board with the cut side nearest you and put a row of carrot strips beside the cut edge. Roll up the omelet tightly and secure the end with a toothpick. Repeat to make a second roll.

6   Cook the sausages according to the package instructions and drain well on paper towels. Cut into ½-inch square sticks. Thickly peel the cucumber and finely shred the skin.

7   Put the canned salmon in a bowl, add the mayonnaise and pinch of salt, and stir well.

8   Following the method on page 14, make 2 sushi rolls with a carrot-and-egg roll filling [remove the toothpicks first], 2 rolls with 1 hot dog or 2 Vienna sausages in a row, and 2 with salmon paste and cucumber shreds.

9   Cut each roll into 6 pieces and serve on a platter with separate dishes of Japanese soy sauce.

Hand-molding of rice is rather a messy job and it's also difficult to make identical shapes and sizes. I have come up with a simple solution, using an egg cup as a mold. These sushi are very easy to make, pretty to serve, and delicious to eat.

egg cup sushi

¼ quantity vinegared rice [page 11]
5–6 smoked salmon slices, about 4 oz.,
   halved to make 10–12 pieces
lemon or lime wedges, to serve

Hand vinegar:
¼ cup Japanese rice vinegar
1 cup water

a small egg cup

Makes 10–12 pieces

1   Make the vinegared rice *[sumeshi]* following the method on page 11. Mix the hand vinegar ingredients in a small bowl and set aside.

2   Line an egg cup with plastic wrap so it hangs over the edge of the cup. Line the whole cup with a piece of smoked salmon, filling any gaps with small pieces of salmon. Put 1 tablespoon of vinegared rice in the cup and press down gently with your thumbs. Do not over-fill. Trim the excess salmon from the rim. Lift up the plastic and turn out the molded sushi, upside down, onto a plate. Repeat to make 10 pieces.

3   Arrange on a serving platter, add lemon or lime wedges, and serve.

Variation:
Make soft scrambled eggs, using 2 eggs, 1 teaspoon sugar, and a pinch of salt. Let cool. Lay a piece of plastic in the egg cup. Put 1 teaspoon of the scrambled eggs on the bottom. Gently press to make a firm base—the egg should come about half way up the side of the cup. Put 1 tablespoon of vinegared rice on top of the egg and again gently press down with your thumbs. Do not over-fill. Using the plastic, turn out the molded sushi, upside down, onto a plate. Repeat this process for the remainder of the egg and rice. Serve with a tiny bit of red caviar on top.

An *inari* is a shrine dedicated to agriculture and the fox is regarded as the envoy of the god. People used to offer *abura-age* [fried tofu] to the fox; hence this special name. This sushi makes an ideal picnic lunch and children's snack.

tofu bags inari-zushi

½ quantity vinegared rice [page 11]
3 fresh Japanese fried tofu *[abura-age]*
¾ cup chicken stock
3 tablespoons sugar
2 tablespoons mirin [rice wine] or
   sweet sherry
2 tablespoons Japanese soy sauce *[shoyu]*
2 dried shiitake mushrooms
2 inches carrot, finely chopped
1 tablespoon sake [optional]

To serve:
pickled ginger
Japanese soy sauce *[shoyu]*

Makes 6 tofu bags

1   Make the vinegared rice *[sumeshi]* following the method on page 11.

2   Put the fried tofu *[abura-age]* on a cutting board and roll each one with a rolling pin. This separates the thin layers inside the tofu, making a bag. Put the tofu in a mixing bowl, pour over boiling water, then drain—this will reduce the oiliness.

3   Cut each piece in half and carefully open each piece from the cut side [if not opened already], to make a bag.

4   Put the chicken stock or water in a saucepan, add 2 tablespoons of the sugar, and bring to a boil. Add the tofu bags, cook 3 minutes on moderate heat, then add 1 tablespoon mirin and 1 tablespoon soy sauce. Simmer over a low heat for about 10 minutes until all the liquid disappears. Remove from the heat and transfer to a plate.

5   Meanwhile, soak the dried shiitake in a bowl of warm water for at least 30 minutes, then drain, reserving the liquid. Cut off the stems and finely chop the caps. Pour ¼ cup of the soaking liquid into a saucepan, add the remaining sugar, mirin, soy sauce, and sake, and bring to a boil. Add the carrot and shiitake and simmer for 3–4 minutes until almost all the liquid is absorbed. Remove from the heat and let cool.

6   While the rice is still warm, fold in the cooked carrot and shiitake. Dip your hands in the hand vinegar and divide the rice mixture into 6 balls. Squeeze out excess juice from the tofu bags and open with your fingers. Stuff a ball of rice into each bag and fold in the edge [optional]. You may cut some bags in half and stuff rice in the corner to make a three-cornered "Napoleon's hat" shape.

7   Arrange the bags on a serving plate and serve with pickled ginger and soy sauce.

SUSHI BAGS

½ quantity vinegared rice [page 11]
10 eggs, beaten
2 tablespoons sugar
½ teaspoon sea salt
1 teaspoon cornstarch blended with
   1 teaspoon water
2 tablespoons sesame seeds [black or white]
2 oz. anchovy fillets, finely chopped
1 bunch of mitzuna [optional]
sunflower oil, for cooking

To serve:
pickled ginger
Japanese soy sauce [shoyu]

Makes 8

1   Make the vinegared rice *[sumeshi]* following the method on page 11.

2   Put the eggs in a large mixing bowl and lightly beat with a fork. Strain through a sieve into another bowl. Add the sugar, salt, and blended cornstarch and mix well until dissolved. Do not whip.

3   Heat an 8-inch skillet, add a little oil, and spread over the base with a paper towel. Add 1 small ladle of the egg mixture and spread evenly over the base by tilting the skillet. Cook over a low heat for about 30 seconds on each side until it becomes firm but not browned. Transfer to a plate and let cool. Repeat to make 8 egg pancakes.

4   Put the sesame seeds in a small saucepan and toss over a moderate heat until they start to pop. Remove from the heat and coarsely crush with a mortar and pestle.

5   While the rice is still warm, fold in the chopped anchovy fillets and crushed sesame seeds. Dip your hands in the hand vinegar, then divide the rice mixture into 8 balls.

6   Put an egg pancake on a board and put a rice ball in the center. Fold the front of the pancake over the rice, then fold over the 2 sides, then the far side, like an envelope. Tuck the edges into the sides. Repeat to make 8 parcels. Alternatively, fold into a money bag, as shown [inset.]

7   If using mitzuna herb to tie the parcels, soak the stems in boiling water for about 30 seconds, using 2 pieces per parcel. Serve with pickled ginger and soy sauce.

Fukusa is an elaborate napkin used for the traditional Japanese tea ceremony. It is folded in various ways and is an important part of the classic performance. It has lent its name to this folded pancake sushi.

omelet parcel sushi fukusa-zushi

2 medium squid, cleaned
3 tablespoons sake
2–3 tablespoons Japanese
   rice vinegar
2 tablespoons sugar
1 tablespoon mirin [rice
   wine] or sweet sherry
2 tablespoons Japanese soy
   sauce [shoyu]
2 oz. ground chicken
   or beef
1 inch fresh ginger, peeled
   and finely chopped
⅔ quantity vinegared rice
   [page 11]
pickled ginger, to serve

Makes 10–12
   pieces

1   Peel the outer skin off the squid. It comes off easily if you hold the two flaps together and peel down the body. Put the 2 main bodies in a saucepan, add 1 tablespoon sake, cover with boiling water, and simmer for 1–2 minutes. Do not overcook. Drain, rub the surface with a damp cloth to remove any marks, then sprinkle with the rice vinegar all over to retain the whiteness. Chop the flaps and tentacles.

2   Put the remaining sake, the sugar, mirin, and soy sauce in a saucepan, mix, and bring to a boil over moderate heat. Add the ground chicken or beef, the chopped squid flaps and tentacles, and the chopped ginger, then stir vigorously with a fork until the meat turns white. Using a slotted spoon, transfer the cooked meat to another bowl, leaving the juice in the saucepan. Boil the juice over high heat for 1–2 minutes until thickened. Stir the meat back into the saucepan to absorb the juice and remove from heat.

3   Make the vinegared rice [sumeshi] following the method on page 11 and, while still warm, fold in the dry-cooked meat. Tightly fill each squid body with half the rice mixture and, using a sharp knife, slice crosswise into 5–6 pieces.

4   Arrange on plates and serve with pickled ginger.

stuffed squid sushi ika-zushi

Meat is rarely used in sushi but this sweet, dry-cooked ground meat goes well with vinegared rice. It can be eaten as it is, or use it as a filling for squid and serve as an unusual party canapé. If you don't like to use meat, just use the squid flaps and tentacles in the sumeshi mixture, but reduce the cooking juice accordingly.

hand-molded sushi nigiri

Hand-molded or *nigiri-zushi* is the king of all sushi. Though it looks simple, it is actually the most difficult to make and is not usually made at home, even in Japan.

⅓ quantity vinegared rice [page 11]

Hand vinegar:
¼ cup Japanese rice vinegar
1 cup water

Toppings:
2 uncooked medium shrimp
1 fillet fresh tuna or salmon,
   about 4 oz., skinned
1 fillet fresh white-fleshed fish, such as fluke,
   flounder, or sole, about 4 oz., skinned
4 oz. squid, cleaned and skinned
2 eggs, beaten
2 tablespoons dashi stock
1 teaspoon mirin [rice wine] or sweet sherry
1 teaspoon Japanese soy sauce [shoyu]
2 teaspoons wasabi paste or powder
2 shiso leaves or basil leaves
a small piece of nori seaweed,
   cut into ⅛-inch strips
salt

To serve:
pickled ginger, to serve
Japanese soy sauce [shoyu]

a sushi rolling mat [makisu]

Makes 8-10 pieces

1   Make the vinegared rice [sumeshi] following the method on page 11. Mix the hand vinegar ingredients in a small bowl and set aside.

2   Skewer a toothpick through each shrimp from top to tail to prevent curling while cooking. Blanch in boiling water for 2 minutes until lightly cooked and pink. Drain and put under running water. Remove and discard the toothpicks, shells, and back vein. Make a slit up the belly lengthwise and open out.

3   Slice the tuna or salmon and sea bream into rectangular pieces, 3 x 1 x ½ inch thick. Cut the squid into similar rectangular pieces and make fine slits on one side of each piece to make the squid more tender.

4   Using the beaten eggs, chicken stock, mirin, and soy sauce, make an omelet following the method on page 60. Put the rolled omelet on a sushi rolling mat and tightly roll into a flat rectangular shape. When cool, cut 2 rectangular pieces, 3 x 1 x ½ inch thick.

5   If using wasabi powder, mix with 2 teaspoons water in an egg cup and stir well to make a clay-like consistency. Leave upside down to prevent drying.

6   Wet your hands in the hand vinegar mixture, take a handful [about 1–2 tablespoons] of the cooked rice in one hand and mold into a rectangular cylinder about 2 x 1 x 1 inch. Put a tiny bit of wasabi on top and cover with an opened shrimp.

7   Repeat, making 2 nigiri topped with shrimp, 2 with tuna or salmon, 2 with sea bream, 2 with squid on top of a shiso leaf, and 2 with omelet. When assembling the nigiri with omelet, do not add wasabi: instead, tie with a thin nori ribbon, about ⅛ inch wide.

8   Arrange on a platter and serve with pickled ginger and Japanese soy sauce in a small dish. Alternatively, serve as party canapés or on small plates as part of a meal.

lettuce boats

½ quantity vinegared rice [page 11]

Hand vinegar:
¼ cup Japanese rice vinegar
1 cup water

Toppings:
4 oz. beef, such as filet mignon, about
   3 inches thick
vegetable oil, for rubbing
1–2 rollmops [marinated Bismarck herring]
8 asparagus tips
2 teaspoons wasabi paste or powder
4 mini romaine lettuce leaves
8 small Belgian endive leaves

To serve:
sprigs of watercress or shredded scallions
a small strip of nori seaweed
1 scallion, finely chopped
1 inch fresh ginger, peeled and grated
2 tablespoons white wine
1½ tablespoons Japanese soy sauce [shoyu]
juice of ½ lemon

Makes 12

1   Make the vinegared rice [sumeshi] following the method on page 11. Mix the hand vinegar ingredients in a small bowl and set aside.

2   Rub the beef all over with vegetable oil. Broil or cook in a stove-top grill pan at a high heat until golden-brown on all sides, but rare in the middle. Plunge into ice water to stop the cooking. Remove from the water, pat dry with paper towels, and cut 4 thin slices, about 3 x 2 inches. All the slices should be red inside and brown around the edges.

3   Cut the rollmops into 4 and make a little lengthwise slit in the skin of each piece.

4   Cook the asparagus in lightly salted water for 5 minutes until soft. Drain and put under running water to arrest cooking and bring out the color. Pat dry with paper towels.

5   If using wasabi powder, mix with 2 teaspoons water in an egg cup, stir to make a clay-like consistency, then turn upside down to stop it drying out.

6   Dip your hands in the hand vinegar and take a handful of the cooked rice in one hand [about 1–2 tablespoons.] Mold it into a rectangular shape about 2 x 1 x 1 inch. Repeat with the remaining rice, making 12 portions. Put a tiny dab of wasabi on top of 4 portions.

7   Arrange a slice of beef on 1 portion of wasabi-and-rice, with the 2 short sides hanging over the end. Top with a few sprigs of cress. Repeat with the other 3 slices of beef and set them in 4 mini romaine lettuce leaves.

8   Arrange 2 asparagus tips on another rice portion and tie with a nori ribbon. Repeat to make 3 more. Arrange a piece of rollmop on each of the remaining 4 rice portions and insert chopped scallion and grated ginger into the slits. Arrange all the leaf boats on a serving platter. Mix the white wine, soy sauce, and the lemon juice in a small bowl. Serve the lettuce boats with a small bowl of lemon sauce and another of plain soy sauce.

Gomoku-zushi means "5-kinds sushi" and usually has 5–8 ingredients. This standard mixture is a popular luncheon dish because it's easy to cook and to adjust the volume and produces a relaxed, friendly atmosphere.

lunchbox sushi mixture

1 quantity vinegared rice [page 11]

Toppings:
3–4 dried shiitake mushrooms
⅓ cup sugar
3 tablespoons Japanese soy sauce *[shoyu]*
½ carrot, finely sliced into 1-inch strips
1 cup chicken stock or water
1 tablespoon sake
2 oz. green beans, trimmed
½ small lotus root *[renkon]* [optional]
¾ cup rice vinegar
2 eggs, beaten
salt
sunflower oil, for cooking

Serves 4-6

1   Soak the shiitake in warm water for 30 minutes. Drain, retaining the soaking liquid. Remove and discard the stems, then thinly slice the caps. Put in a small saucepan, cover with ½ cup soaking liquid, 2 tablespoons sugar, and 2 tablespoons soy sauce. Simmer for 10 minutes or until most of the liquid disappears. Transfer to a bowl and let cool.

2   Put the finely sliced carrot in the saucepan with water to cover. Bring to a boil, then drain in a colander. Put the chicken stock or water in the saucepan, add the remaining soy sauce and sake, bring to a boil, add the carrot, and cook for 3–4 minutes. Transfer to a bowl and let cool.

3   Add some lightly salted water to the saucepan, bring to a boil, add the beans and boil for 2 minutes until just soft. Drain and cool under running water. Pat dry with paper towels and slice diagonally into 2-inch long shreds.

4   Peel the lotus root, if using, and slice into thin rings. Bring a small saucepan of water to a boil, add 1 tablespoon rice vinegar and the lotus root, and boil until just soft. Drain and transfer to a mixing bowl. Put the remaining rice vinegar in the saucepan, add the remaining sugar and 2 teaspoons salt, bring to a boil, and stir until dissolved. Remove from the heat, add to the lotus root, and let marinate for 15–20 minutes.

5   Beat the eggs with a pinch of salt. Heat an 8-inch skillet, brush with sunflower oil, add the egg, and cook until just set. Transfer the egg pancake to a cutting board and cut into fine shreds, 2 inches long.

6   Make the vinegared rice *[sumeshi]* following the recipe on page 11. Put the rice in a bowl and fold in all the ingredients except the egg shreds and a few of the beans. Transfer to bowls or lunchboxes, top with the egg shreds and beans, and serve.

½ quantity vinegared rice
[page 11]

Sashimi [your choice of]:
2 uncooked medium shrimp,
  peeled but with tail fins
  intact
1 octopus tentacle
4 oz. fresh tuna and/or
  salmon
1 grouper or bass fillet,
  about 3 oz.
1 small squid, cleaned and
  skinned
2 large dried shiitake
  mushrooms
1 teaspoon sugar
1 teaspoon mirin [rice wine]
salt

To serve:
2 inches cucumber
pink pickled ginger
wasabi paste
Japanese soy sauce [shoyu]

Serves 2

1   Make the vinegared rice [sumeshi] following the method on page 11.

2   Bring a saucepan of lightly salted water to a boil, add the shrimp and poach for 1–2 minutes until just pink. Remove with a slotted spoon, cool under running water, then pat dry with paper towels.

3   Return the pan of water to a boil, add the octopus tentacle, and cook for 7–8 minutes. Drain and cool under running water. Pat dry with paper towels and slice diagonally into thin disks.

4   Cut the fish into 4 slices each.

5   Put the squid, skin side up, on a cutting board and make very fine slits two-thirds of the way through the thickness, first lengthwise, then crosswise. Put in a bowl, pour over boiling water, and drain. As the squid curls up, the slits open to form a flower. Immediately plunge into cold water. Pat dry with paper towels and cut into 4 bite size pieces.

6   Soak the shiitake in warm water for 30 minutes and drain, retaining the soaking liquid. Cut off the stems and put in a saucepan with the sugar, mirin, and a pinch of salt. Cover with some of the soaking liquid, stir, then bring to a boil and simmer for 4–5 minutes until most of the liquid disappears. Let cool in the liquid.

7   Cut 2 green slices off the cucumber, 2 inches wide. Make fine slits lengthwise, leaving ½ inch intact on one side. Open up the slits to make 2 cucumber fans.

8   Divide the rice between 2 bowls and arrange the seafood over the rice and top with a cucumber fan and a pile of pink pickled ginger. Serve on small individual plates with a tiny heap of wasabi, and a little pitcher of soy sauce.

sushi in a bowl edomae chirashi-zushi

A bowl of sushi with sashimi on top is a favorite in Tokyo. You can use just one ingredient like tuna, or the assorted sashimi normally used in restaurants including tuna, shrimp, eel, sea bass, shellfish, herring roe, salmon roe-almost any good material from the market on the day. My selection is good for serving at home.

1 quantity vinegared rice [page 11]

Radish petals:
4–5 radishes, trimmed
2 tablespoons rice vinegar
2 tablespoons sugar

Egg petals:
1 egg, beaten
¼ teaspoon cornstarch mixed with a little water
sunflower oil, for cooking

Your choice of:
5 dried shiitake mushrooms
⅓ cup sugar
2½ tablespoons mirin [rice wine]
1 teaspoon Japanese soy sauce [shoyu]
¼ cup chicken stock
½ carrot, sliced into 1-inch matchsticks
1 oz. snowpeas, trimmed
3 oz. cod fillet
1 tablespoon sake
red food coloring [optional]
3 tablespoons white sesame seeds, lightly
    toasted in a dry skillet
8 oz. small shrimp, peeled and lightly cooked
salt

flower cutters or a small sharp knife

Serves 4–6

tub of spring sushi

1   Make the vinegared rice *[sumeshi]* following the method on page 11.

2   Cut a wedge out of each radish, then slice each radish crosswise to form 5–6 petal shapes. Put the rice vinegar and sugar in a bowl and stir well until sugar has dissolved. Add the radish slices and marinate for a few hours or overnight. The red color dissolves into the vinegar, making the slices cherry pink.

3   Mix the egg in a bowl with a pinch of salt and the blended cornstarch. Heat a small skillet, brush with sunflower oil, add the egg mixture, and cook until set. Using molds or a small knife, cut out small shapes from the egg pancake such as hearts or petals.

4   Soak the shiitake in warm water for 30 minutes, then drain, retaining the soaking liquid. Discard the stems and thinly slice the caps crosswise. Put the shiitake slices, ½ cup from the soaking liquid, and 2 tablespoons of the sugar in a saucepan, bring to a boil, and cook for 3–4 minutes. Add the mirin and soy sauce, then simmer until the liquid disappears.

5   Put the chicken stock in a saucepan, add ½ teaspoon of the sugar, a pinch of salt, and the carrot. Bring to a boil and cook for 2–3 minutes until just soft. Let cool in the juice.

6   Blanch the snowpeas in lightly salted water. Slice diagonally into diamonds.

7   Bring a saucepan of water to a boil, add the cod, simmer for 3–4 minutes, then drain. Carefully remove the skin and all the bones. Return to a dry saucepan, add 1 tablespoon sake, the remaining sugar, and a pinch of salt. Finely flake over a low heat, using a fork. If using red coloring, dilute it in a little water, then quickly stir to make the fish flakes light pink.

8   While the rice is still warm, fold in the shiitake, carrot matchsticks, flaked fish, shrimp, and sesame seeds. Top with the radish and egg "petals" and serve.

Absolutely fresh fish is vital for sashimi. Buy from a retailer that specifies "sashimi-grade" or "sushi-grade" fish. Wherever possible, instead of buying ready-cut fillets, buy whole fish and ask the fishmonger to fillet it for you. With big fish, such as tuna or salmon, fillets are fine.

classic sashimi

1 fillet white fish such as fluke, flounder, or sole
2 small fresh mackerel fillets
1 slice of lemon, cut into 8 fan-shaped wedges
6 oz. tuna
6 oz. salmon fillet
1 small squid, cleaned and skinned
2 inches large daikon [white radish], peeled
4 shiso leaves [optional]

To serve:
4 teaspoons wasabi paste or powder [page 62]
Japanese soy sauce [shoyu]

Serves 4

1   To skin the fillets, put them on a cutting board, skin side down. Hold down the skin of the tail with your fingers, then run the blade along the skin, separating the flesh. Cut the whole fillet lengthwise along the center line. Insert the blade diagonally against the cutting board and slice each fillet crosswise into 8 pieces, ½-inch thick. Make a slit in each piece and insert a fan-shaped piece of lemon.

2   Salt and vinegar the mackerel following the method on page 30. Slice the fillets into ½-inch pieces, as above.

3   Slice the tuna and salmon into 8 pieces, 2 x 1 inch, about ½ inch thick.

4   Cut the squid into 8 pieces and finely slice each piece lengthwise, leaving the pieces attached at one end.

5   Using a mandoline or sharp knife, finely shred the daikon. Put the shreds in a bowl of ice water for about 30 minutes to make them crisp. Drain and pat dry with paper towels.

6   To serve, put a mound of daikon shreds, a small mound of wasabi paste, and a shiso leaf, if using, on each plate. Add 2 slices of each fish and serve with a small dish of Japanese soy sauce.

SASHIMI
RECIPES

seared tuna sashimi salad

It may take time to get used to the idea of eating completely raw fish, but lightly blanched or seared fillet with salad is a good starting point. You can use other fish such as salmon.

8 oz. fresh tuna or
  swordfish, skinned
green salad leaves
a small clump of enoki
  mushrooms, trimmed
  and separated

Wasabi dressing:
juice of 1 lemon
2 teaspoons wasabi paste
1½ tablespoons Japanese
  soy sauce *[shoyu]*

Serves 4

1 Cook the tuna or swordfish on a stove-top grill pan at a high heat for about 1 minute on each side until the surfaces are seared but the inside is still raw. Plunge into ice water. Drain and pat dry with paper towels. Slice into ⅛-inch thick pieces.

2 Mix the lemon juice, wasabi, and soy sauce in a small bowl and set aside.

3 Arrange the salad leaves and enoki mushrooms in the center of a large serving plate and arrange the seared fish over the leaves. Just before serving, pour the wasabi dressing over the top.

japanese omelet
tamago yaki

This is the basic method for cooking Japanese omelet. It is a regular breakfast item as well as being used for sushi.

4 eggs
1 egg yolk
2½ tablespoons sugar
1 teaspoon Japanese soy sauce
[shoyu]
salt
1–2 tablespoons sunflower oil

1 Japanese omelet pan or
8-inch nonstick skillet

Makes 1 omelet

1   Using a fork, beat the eggs and egg yolk and strain through a sieve into a bowl. Add the sugar, soy sauce, and pinch of salt and stir well until the sugar has dissolved. Do not whisk or make bubbles.

2   Heat a Japanese omelet pan or skillet over moderate heat and add a little oil. Spread evenly over the base by tilting the pan, then wipe off excess oil with paper towels, at the same time making sure the surface is absolutely smooth. Keep the oiled paper on a plate.

3   Lower the heat and pour one-third of the egg mixture evenly over the base by tilting the pan. If large air bubbles pop up immediately, the pan may be too hot—then remove the pan from the heat and put it back on when the egg starts to set.

4   Prick any air bubbles with a fork and, when the egg is about to set, using chopsticks or a fork, roll the egg layer 2–3 times from one side to the other. Oil the empty base of the pan with the oiled paper and push the rolled egg back to the other side.

5   Again using the oiled paper, brush the base of the pan, then pour half the remaining egg mixture evenly over the base by tilting the pan and lifting the egg roll so the egg mixture flows underneath.

6   When the egg starts to set, roll again, using the first roll as the core. Repeat this oiling and rolling using up the remaining egg mixture. Remove from the pan and let cool before cutting.

BASIC
RECIPES

wasabi—japanese horseradish

Freshly grated wasabi root, available in Japan, is divine. However ready-made wasabi pastes are now so good that many restaurants, even in Japan, use them rather than laboring to grate fresh ones. Pastes are sold in tubes, and powder in cans. Tubes are handy to use but freshly made paste from powder has more kick and better flavor.

1 Put 1 teaspoon wasabi powder in an egg cup and add 1 teaspoon of water. Stir vigorously with a teaspoon to make a clay-like consistency. Turn the egg cup upside-down to keep the wasabi moist until serving.

Makes enough for 10 pieces rolled sushi

pickled ginger

1 teaspoon salt
4 oz. fresh ginger, peeled
¼ cup rice vinegar
1¼ tablespoons sugar

Makes about 1½ cups

Gari is sushi shop jargon for pickled ginger slices. It is always served with sushi and sashimi. It is delicious to eat and also works as a mouth freshener.

1 Rub the salt into the ginger and leave overnight. Drain and wipe with paper towels.

2 Mix the rice vinegar, sugar, and 3½ tablespoons water in a mixing bowl. Stir until dissolved, add the ginger and set aside to marinate for 1 week. Alternatively, finely slice the ginger, blanch for 2 minutes, then marinate as before. It is ready to use when it turns slightly pink. Store in an airtight container in the fridge—it keeps for several months.

3 To serve, remove from the marinade and slice very thinly along the grain.

DIRECTORY

MAIL ORDER

ANZEN IMPORTS
736 N. E. Union Avenue,
Portland, OR 97232
Tel 503-233-5111

CENTRAL MARKET
40th & Lamar Streets,
Austin, TX 7656
Tel 800-360-2552
Website www.centralmarket.com

CMC COMPANY
P.O.Drawer 322,
Avalon, NJ 08202
Tel 800-CMC-2780
Website www.thecmccompany.com

FREMONT FINE FOOD
7901 4th Street NW
Albuquerque, NM 87110
Tel 505-792-3463

JASMINE ORIENTAL MART
1504 A Bloomingdale Road,
Glendale Heights, IL 60137
Tel 630-682-3011

KAM MAN FOODS
200 Canal Street,
New York, NY 10013
Tel 212-766-9085

KATAGIRI
224 East 59th Street,
New York, NY 10022
Tel 212 755 3566
Website www.katagiri.com

ORIENTAL PANTRY
423 Great Road,
Acton, MA 01/20
Tel 800-828-0368
Website www.orientalpantry.com

THE SPICE HOUSE
1031 N. Old World 3rd Street,
Milwaukee, WI 53203
Tel 414-272-0977
Website www.thespicehouse.com

UWAJIMAYA
519 Sixth Avenue,
South Seattle, WA 98104
Tel 800-889-1928
Website www.uwajimaya.com

Stores that do not offer mail order services but sell sushi ingredients

ANN'S ORIENTAL GROCERY
315 Arvada Street
Colorado Springs, CO 80906
Tel 719-597-0244

BEACON MARKET
2500 Beacon Street
Seattle, WA 98144
Tel 206 323 2050

DOBASHI MARKET, INC.
240 East Jackson Street
San Jose, CA 95112
Tel 408-295-7794

FUTABA FOOD CENTER
1507 Lincoln Avenue
Pasadena, CA 91103
Tel 626 797 0466

INDEX